Ortho Easy-Step Books

Roses

*Created and designed
by the editorial staff of
Ortho Books*

Contents

Introduction   **4**

Using Roses in the Garden   **7**
  1 Choose the site
  2 Select plant shape and size
  3 Consider key characteristics
  4 Understand patents
  5 Decide where to buy
  6 Purchase healthy plants

Planting for Best Growth   **17**
  1 Provide drainage
  2 Prepare the soil
  3 Plant bare-root roses
  4 Plant container-grown types
  5 Plant tree varieties
  6 Plant and support climbers
  7 Transplant dormant roses
  8 Grow roses in containers

Caring for Roses   **29**
  1 Mulch under plants
  2 Water deeply
  3 Apply fertilizer
  4 Deter and control pests
  5 Combat diseases
  6 Protect from severe weather

Pruning the Plants   41

1 Know when to prune
2 Decide where to cut
3 Prune bush roses
4 Cut back climbers
5 Shape tree varieties
6 Prune container plants

More Information   50

- Using roses as cut flowers
- A glossary of rose terms
- Roses for special purposes
- U.S./metric measure conversions

Gardeners have been growing roses for hundreds of years, in many parts of the world. Few flowers can match the rose in beauty or fragrance, nor offer as many flower colors. Rose plants can be small, treelike, or cover a fence. They can be used for different purposes throughout the garden, adding both beauty and color to the landscape. This book will help you select healthy roses and plant them properly. It will guide you as you care for them, including watering, mulching, and fertilizing. Pruning, an especially important part of rose care, is also covered.

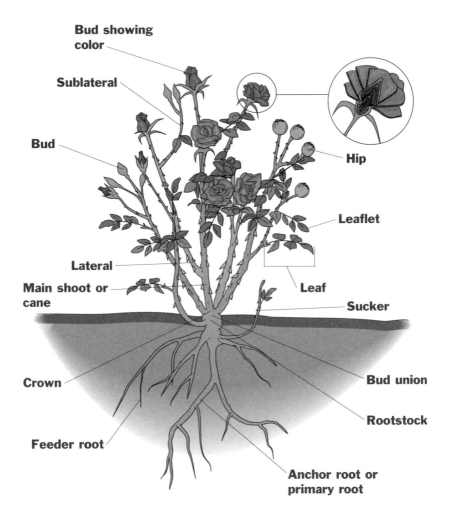

Bud showing color

Sublateral

Bud

Hip

Leaflet

Lateral

Main shoot or cane

Leaf

Sucker

Crown

Bud union

Rootstock

Feeder root

Anchor root or primary root

Using Roses in the Garden

1 Choose the site

Plant roses where they receive at least six hours of full sun a day, with some shade in the afternoon in areas with intense summer heat. Roses also need good air circulation. Avoid sites with strong winds, or protect the roses by planting or building windbreaks. Roses will grow in most soil, but do best in well-drained, slightly acid soil. Don't plant roses too close to trees or shrubs whose roots will compete with them for water and nutrients. For added enjoyment, plant roses where they can be viewed from inside your home.

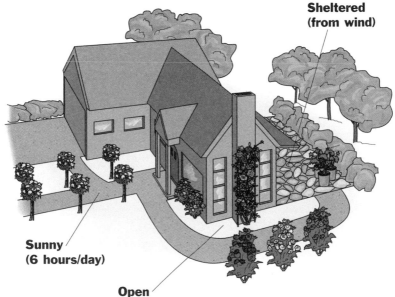

Sheltered (from wind)

Sunny (6 hours/day)

Open (no competing plants)

T I P : Plant rose-bushes at least 2 feet back from walkways so thorny branches won't snag passersby.

Select plant shape and size

The main categories of modern roses are miniatures, floribundas, hybrid teas, grandifloras, tree roses, and climbers. Miniature roses usually grow 6 to 18 inches tall and are used in containers and for edging, low borders, and ground cover. Floribundas bear many clusters of medium-sized flowers and are from 2 to 5 feet tall. They are hardy and usually bloom continuously from late spring through fall. Use them in containers and for borders, hedges, and ground cover.

Miniature   **Floribunda**   **Hybrid tea**

Hybrid tea roses are the most widely grown rose type. They normally grow from 4 to 5 feet tall and have large, fragrant, single flowers on long stems. Grandifloras grow to 6 feet or more and produce clusters of fairly large flowers. Tree roses (sometimes known as standard roses) have a slender trunk and a flowering top. Climbing roses grow from 6 to 20 feet tall, usually on a fence, post, or trellis. They are divided into two groups: large-flowered climbers, which have rigid, thick canes, and ramblers, which have thinner, flexible canes.

Grandiflora   **Tree rose**   **Climber**

Consider key characteristics

Along with their shape and size, there are several other factors to consider when choosing a rose. Select varieties that grow best in your climate and whose fragrance and color you enjoy. Consider the amount of maintenance the plant needs and its resistance to disease. If you plan to grow your roses for cut flowers, remember that all roses can be picked for indoor arrangements, but hybrid teas and grandifloras are most often used because of their long, straight stems.

Prepare a checklist before you shop.

Understand patents

Before a new rose is introduced to the public, it is named and patented. The patent holder receives a small percentage from the sale of each plant until the patent expires. The patents on many excellent roses have expired, so these nonpatented plants are slightly less expensive. New roses are tested over a two-year period to judge their overall quality. Under the direction of the All-America Rose Selections (AARS), each rose is rated. Yearly award winners are listed in mail-order catalogs and on their name tags at nurseries.

Rose
English Rose
ORTHELLO
(AUSLO)
U.S. PL PAT.
No. 7212

T I P : Don't buy roses sold as patented unless they carry a patent number engraved on the tag.

Decide where to buy

Nurseries and mail-order companies are the two most common sources for roses. Local nurseries usually stock varieties that do well in the area, and you can choose the specific plants you want. Nursery personnel can also provide advice. You can't personally select the plants you buy from mail-order companies, but it is a convenient way to shop. Some of these catalogs are the best sources for the largest selection of the newest varieties as well as old or unusual ones that are seldom available locally.

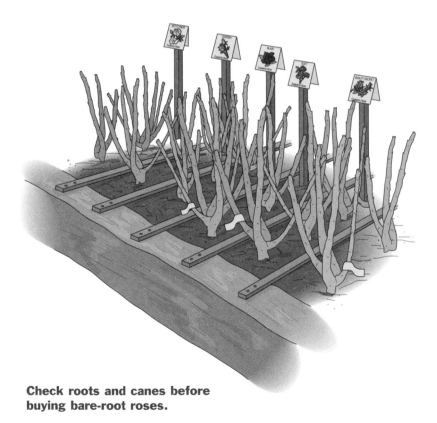

Check roots and canes before buying bare-root roses.

Place your order early to be sure you receive your first choices. If appropriate, list a few substitutions that you would accept. Many mail-order growers have cool-storage facilities that allow them to ship your roses at the best planting time for your area. Plant them as soon as they arrive. If that is not possible, place the bare roots in moist peat moss or sawdust or in a trench in the ground. Keep the tops of the plants cool so they do not begin to sprout before being planted.

Storing Bare-Root Plants

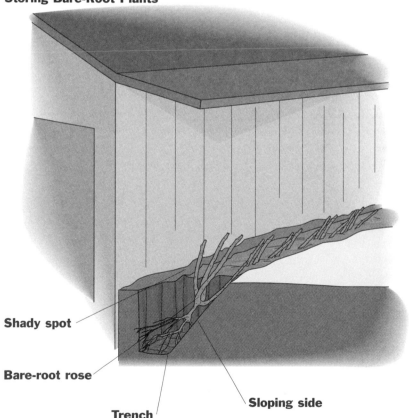

Shady spot

Bare-root rose

Trench

Sloping side

6 Purchase healthy plants

You will be investing a lot of time and energy in each rose you purchase, so spend a little extra money for high-quality plants. When buying container-grown roses, examine the foliage and canes carefully. They should look healthy and vigorous, with no evidence of pests or disease. It is best to buy plants grown in 3- or 5-gallon cans. Miniature roses are usually sold in smaller containers and can be purchased at any time of year. Select miniatures with healthy green foliage that is not tangled.

Select container plants with thick canes, healthy, green leaves, and vigorous root systems.

Bare-root roses are graded #1, #1½, or #2, based on the size, number, and distribution of their canes and the quality of their root system. It is best to buy #1 grade plants. Look for plump, firm, green canes and sturdy, fibrous, and well-branched roots. Buy plants before they begin to leaf out. If they have already sprouted, pinch back the leaf shoots to ¼ inch long. If the entire rose is wrapped in plastic, remove the wrapping as soon as you get home.

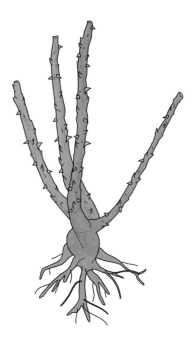

Choose bare-root roses with strong canes and roots, and a symmetrical shape.

Planting for Best Growth

Provide drainage

If your soil does not drain well, mix in compost and/or gypsum. If you are preparing a large rose bed, provide drainage by digging a trench and burying drain tile or drainage pipe in coarse gravel 12 to 15 inches beneath the planting site. Cover the drain openings with filter cloth to prevent soil from washing in. Slightly slant the pipe toward a ditch, storm sewer, or dry well. Or build a raised bed at least 16 to 20 inches high, with sides made of redwood or masonry framing, railroad ties, stone, or brick. Fill the bed with amended soil.

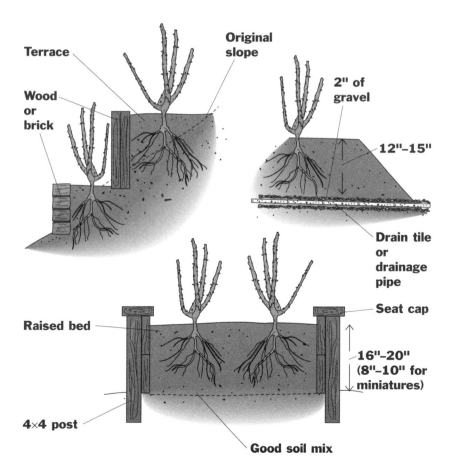

Terrace

Wood or brick

Original slope

2" of gravel

12"–15"

Drain tile or drainage pipe

Raised bed

Seat cap

16"–20" (8"–10" for miniatures)

4×4 post

Good soil mix

Prepare the soil

Roses grow well in many kinds of soil, but they do best in loamy soil with a high humus content to a depth of at least 2 feet, and a pH (the level of acidity or alkalinity) of 6.0 to 6.5. You can buy a pH test kit, or have the soil tested by a laboratory. The lab or your nursery can provide information on how to raise or lower the pH if necessary.

Remove debris.

If you're planting a few bushes individually and the soil is good, dig large planting holes and plant as described on pages 20 to 26. If you're preparing a new area to be planted, first remove any weeds, stones, or debris. Till or dig the soil at least 12 inches deep, spread a 2- to 3-inch layer of organic material and/or gypsum evenly over the planting bed, and till it again.

12"

Till in organic matter.

Plant bare-root roses

Soak the roots in water for two to three hours. Dig a hole at least 18 inches deep by 18 inches wide. Add compost, aged manure, or gypsum to the excavated soil. Make a cone-shaped mound at the bottom of the hole with about half the soil mixture. Trim off any long or broken roots from the rose. Place the plant in the hole, spreading the roots over the mound. Check the plant's depth: The bud union should be 1 to 2 inches above ground level in warm climates, and 1 to 2 inches below ground in areas with severe winters.

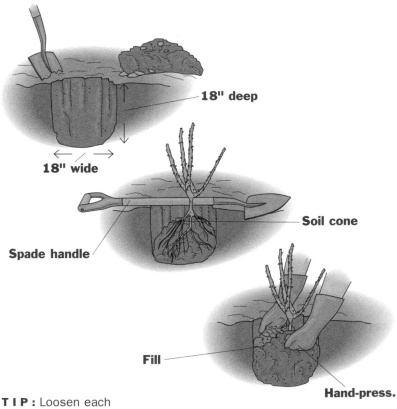

18" deep

18" wide

Soil cone

Spade handle

Fill

Hand-press.

TIP: Loosen each plant's label so it does not constrict the cane.

Fill the hole two thirds full with the enriched soil, tamping it gently. Fill with water and let it soak in. Finish filling the hole with soil, firm it by hand, and settle it with a second soaking. Mound 6 inches of soil around and over the canes and moisten it again. When new growth at the tips of the canes is 1 to 2 inches long and all danger of frost has passed, gently wash away a bit of the mounded soil each day.

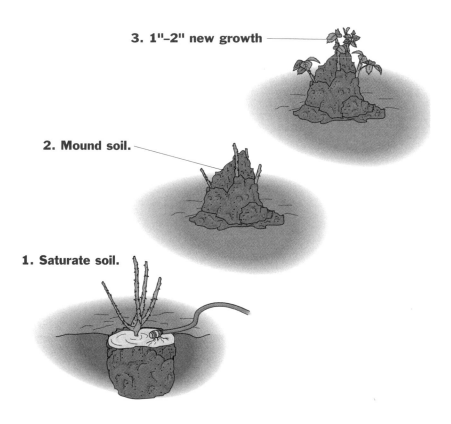

3. 1"–2" new growth

2. Mound soil.

1. Saturate soil.

4 Plant container-grown types

Dig a hole as deep as, and 5 to 6 inches wider than, the container in which the rose is growing. In hard-to-work soil, loosen it 6 to 8 inches deeper, leaving that loose soil in the hole. Mix amendments into the excavated soil. Carefully remove the plant from its container and gently loosen the roots on the sides of the rootball. Position the bud union correctly (see page 20) and add soil, lightly firming it by hand. Water thoroughly to settle it, fill the hole with additional soil, and water again.

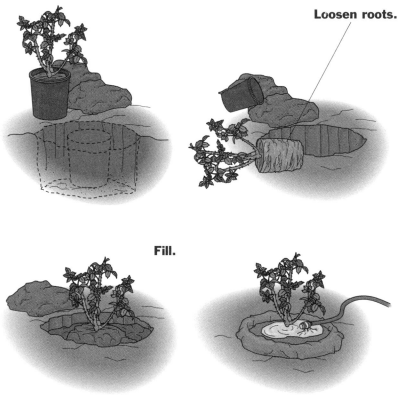

Loosen roots.

Fill.

Water.

Plant tree varieties

Tree roses can be planted bare root or from containers in the same way bush roses are. Plant them in protected locations, because they cannot tolerate strong wind. Before planting, install a 1-inch by 1-inch stake on the side of the prevailing wind. Plant the rose next to the stake, and drive the stake into the ground about 1 foot, so that the top of it is just above the bud union. Secure the stake to the trunk with plant tape wrapped in a figure-eight pattern.

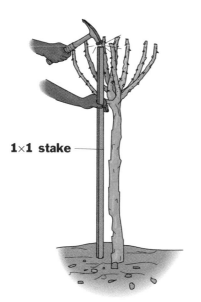

1×1 stake

Bud union

T I P : Don't tighten the ties fully until the plant has settled into the soil. Loosen the ties as the diameter of the trunk increases.

6

Plant and support climbers

Plant bare-root or container-grown climbers as you would bush roses. Although a newly planted climber may appear to be short, tie it onto its support immediately by carefully spreading out and securing the branches. One of the best ways to support climbers on a wall is with plastic-coated wire secured with tapered vine eyes or strong nails. String the wires horizontally, about 15 inches apart, and drive the vine eyes or nails every 6 to 8 feet. Pull the wire taut before securing it to the next eye.

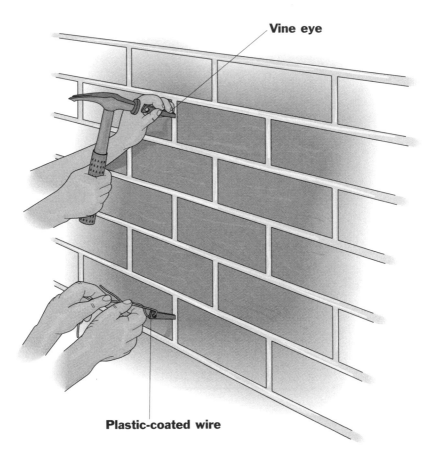

Vine eye

Plastic-coated wire

Use plastic strips, string, or burlap to attach young climbing branches to whatever support system you use. Don't tie too tightly—allow room for the shoots to grow. Let the canes grow long and then arch or tie them in a horizontal position with the tips of the canes pointed downward. This will stimulate more flowers to form along the stems. If the lower portions of the stems lose their leaves, shorten some of the long upright canes to stimulate the growth of side shoots.

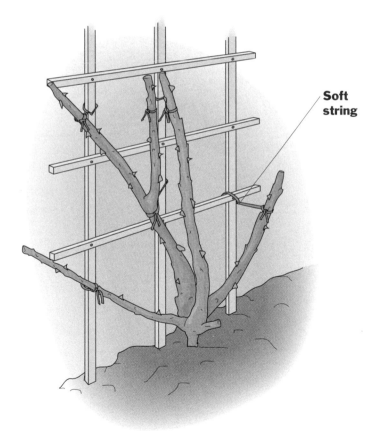

Soft string

7 Transplant dormant roses

Transplant an established rose when it is dormant and the ground is workable. Soak the soil around the plant a day before transplanting so the plant can be moved with as much soil as possible. Prune back large bushes by at least one half. Prepare the new planting site as for a container-grown rose (see page 22). Move the rose to its new location and replant it right away. Position it in the hole and firm the soil around the roots. Water it well and keep it moist until the roots are established.

Old location
(rose has been pruned back)

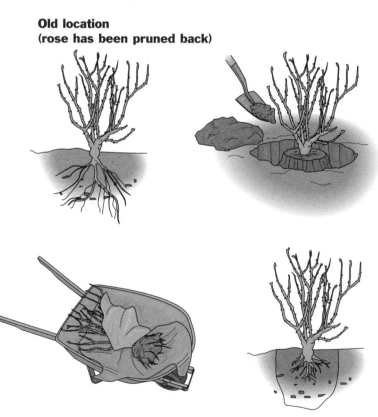

New location

8

Grow roses in containers

Select a container that will give the root system room to grow. It must have drainage holes. Cover them with broken crockery or screen to prevent soil from washing out. Place the container on casters, feet, wood *x*'s, or pieces of brick to help air circulate underneath it. Add a few scoops of potting soil and set the plant at the correct height—as if you were planting it in the ground (see page 20). Fill and water, leaving about 2 inches between the soil level and the top of the pot.

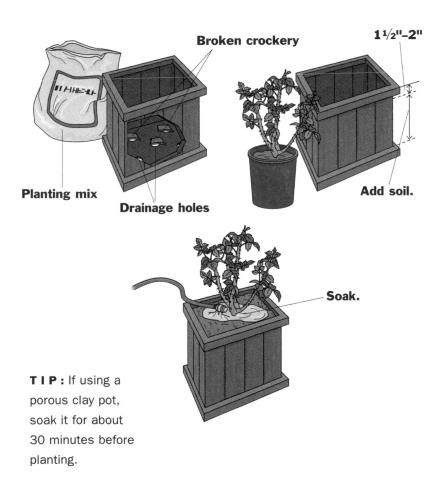

Broken crockery

1 1/2"–2"

Planting mix

Drainage holes

Add soil.

Soak.

T I P : If using a porous clay pot, soak it for about 30 minutes before planting.

Caring for Roses

1 Mulch under plants

Spread mulch on top of the soil to prevent weeds, insulate the soil, and give the rose bed a neat appearance. Use bark, compost, or gravel 2 to 4 inches deep. Weed-blocking fabric can be placed on the soil underneath the mulch. This allows water through but blocks the light needed by weed seeds to grow. Do not let mulch mound up around the base of the plants. Where fungus diseases are a problem, remove the mulch yearly in early fall and replace it with fresh material.

Mulching Materials

Bark Available in chip form or finely ground. Attractive and long lasting.

Sawdust, wood chips, or wood shavings Low in plant nutrients; decompose slowly; tend to pack down. Keep away from building foundations—may attract termites.

Grass clippings or hay Often readily available, but unattractive. Let dry before spreading. Repeated use builds up reserve of nutrients which lasts for years.

Gravel Not too attractive with roses. Very durable, holds down weeds, but does not supply nutrients or humus.

Newspaper Can be shredded or used as sheets, and held in place by rocks, bricks, or soil. Cover with more-attractive material. Builds humus.

Pine needles Will not mat down. Fairly durable. Can be a fire hazard. Increases soil acidity over time.

Rotted manure High in salts, so make sure it is well rotted. May contain weed seeds if obtained from a farm or stable. Can be purchased heat-treated.

Straw Long lasting. Depletes nitrogen when worked into the soil, but adds potassium. Use a fertilizer high in nitrogen with it.

Tree leaves (whole or shredded) Excellent source of humus. Rots rapidly; high in nutrients.

Weed-blocking fabric Discourages weeds while allowing water in. Can be covered with a thin layer of bark or other material for a better appearance.

Water deeply

Roses need deep, consistent watering. Give a rose 1 to 2 inches of water a week, all at one time, from early spring through fall. More water is needed when the soil is sandy and loose, when the air is hot and dry, or when the roses are newly planted. The soil should be soaked to a depth of 1½ feet. Test for water penetration by using a small shovel or a moisture tester with a long probe. Keep roses in containers well watered—check their soil often to make sure it isn't too dry.

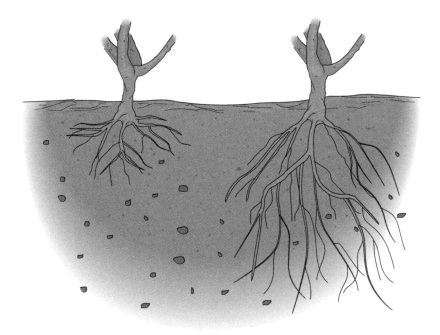

Deep watering encourages a strong root system.

Use drip irrigation or underground sprinklers, or water by hand. The most efficient method is a drip emitter system, which applies water slowly without runoff. Place one emitter on each side of a rosebush, use manufactured drip collars, or make your own collars with perforated tubing or tubing joined with in-line emitters. If you have an underground system with spray heads, use it early in the morning so the leaves will have time to dry before evening. Use bubbler attachments on hoses or on underground sprinkler systems to slowly soak the soil.

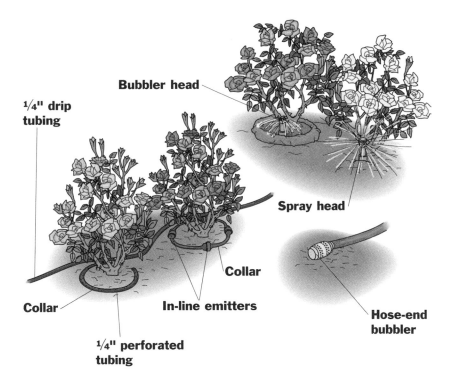

Bubbler head

¼" drip tubing

Spray head

Collar

In-line emitters

Collar

Hose-end bubbler

¼" perforated tubing

Apply fertilizer

Most roses need regular applications of fertilizer. Plants growing in sandy soil need more frequent applications; those in heavier soils may not need as many. Both natural organic and synthetic fertilizers are available in dry or liquid forms. Work dry fertilizers into the top 1 to 2 inches of moistened soil—several inches away from the base of the plant and out to the edge of the foliage. Water in. Liquid fertilizers are added to water and usually applied to the roots. Foliar liquid fertilizers are sprayed onto the leaves, which absorb the nutrients.

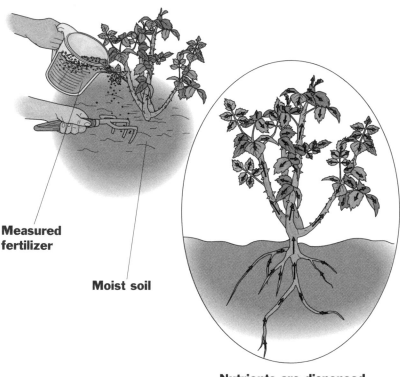

Measured fertilizer

Moist soil

Nutrients are dispensed through the entire plant.

Always follow label directions, applying the recommended amount. Begin fertilizing newly planted roses about three to four weeks after planting. Fertilize older plants after they have been pruned heavily in winter or early spring and the new foliage has started to grow. Fertilize again every six to eight weeks, or three to four times during the growing season. For roses in containers, cut the recommended dosage in half and apply it twice as often. If you use too much, soak the soil several times to wash out the excess.

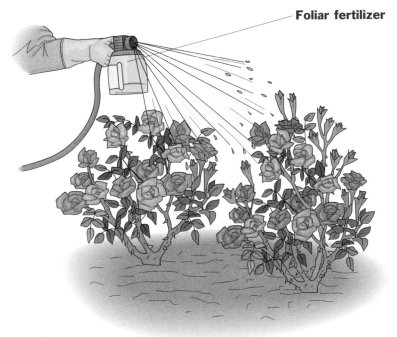

Foliar fertilizer

TIP: Do not spray fertilizer on foliage on hot days.

4 Deter and control pests

Prevent pest damage by choosing resistant rose varieties, planting them properly, and giving them the best care. Remove clippings and dead material from the plant and surrounding soil as soon as possible, as they are good hiding places for pests. Inspect the roses regularly. Be sure to look under the leaves. Infestations caught early can be controlled by spraying with a natural pest-control product, or a solution of 1 teaspoon of a mild dishwashing detergent mixed in 1 gallon of water. Repeat this treatment every three days until the insects are gone.

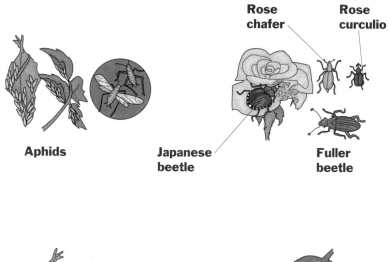

Rose chafer

Rose curculio

Aphids

Japanese beetle

Fuller beetle

Budworm and other caterpillars

Leafhoppers

Purchase beneficial insects such as the ladybird beetle, praying mantis, Trichogramma wasp, and lace wing to help keep aphids and certain other pests under control. If needed, apply chemical sprays, granules, or dusts, following label directions for dosage and intervals. Water plants well the day before spraying, mix chemicals in a ventilated area, and spray on a calm day to prevent drift. Wear protective clothing and avoid inhaling any chemical. Wash up well after handling pesticides.

Rose midge

Rose scales

Spider mites

Thrips

Combat diseases

Buying high-quality, disease-resistant plants is the best way to prevent common diseases. Keep the rose bed clean of weeds and fallen leaves.

Do a winter cleanup while the plants are dormant so diseases won't overwinter in the debris. To keep rust and black spot from carrying over from year to year, strip all leaves from the bushes in the winter—even in warm-winter areas. Rake up and discard any fallen leaves. Spray the plant and soil with a mixture of fungicide and dormant oil spray.

Black spot

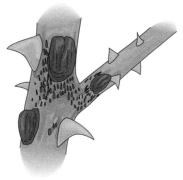

Canker

Crown gall

Some diseases can be prevented by watering correctly. Do overhead watering only in the morning. When hand-watering, use a hose-end bubbler to prevent splashing. Remove and destroy all canes showing cankers or discolored sunken spots. Remove leaves with black spots or orange-colored rust spores as soon as you see them. You can control many diseases by applying a fungicide during the growing season. Choose one specific to the disease present. When mixing, applying, or disposing of fungicides, follow all label instructions and warnings.

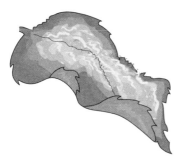

Powdery mildew

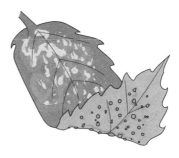

Rust

**Virus disease
(including mosaic)**

6 Protect from severe weather

Move container roses to partially shaded locations when it is extremely hot, and into an unheated shelter away from chilling winds in cold climates. Keep them moist during the winter, but do not fertilize. In mild-winter climates, no special protection is needed for bush or tree roses. Just mulch the soil and cut back on the fertilizer and water. In cold-winter areas, mound compost or fresh, well-draining soil (from another area of the garden) 6 to 8 inches high at the base of each plant after the first hard frost.

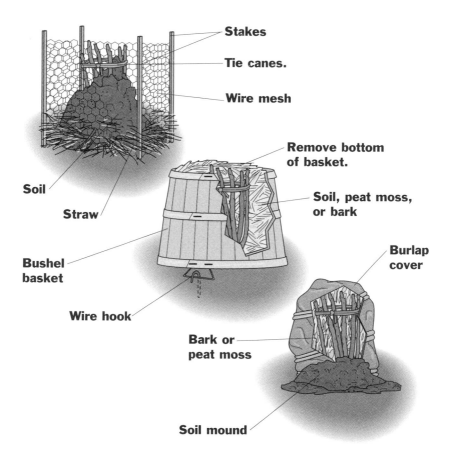

Stakes

Tie canes.

Wire mesh

Remove bottom of basket.

Soil, peat moss, or bark

Soil

Straw

Bushel basket

Wire hook

Burlap cover

Bark or peat moss

Soil mound

A wire-mesh cylinder supported by three or four stakes will insulate the roses. Prune them so they don't whip around in the wind. Fill the cylinder loosely with shredded bark, straw, or evergreen boughs. In the spring remove the cylinder and this material and give the plants their annual winter pruning. The tops of tree roses can be packed with straw, covered with burlap, and loosely tied with twine. Do the same with climbing-rose canes but add a foot or more of soil mounded over the canes at the base of the plants.

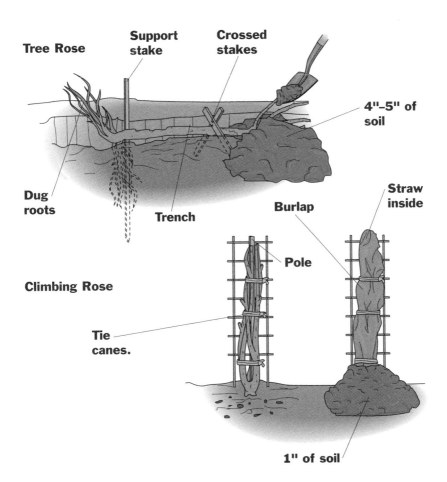

Tree Rose   **Support stake**   **Crossed stakes**

4"–5" of soil

Dug roots   **Trench**   **Burlap**   **Straw inside**

Pole

Climbing Rose

Tie canes.

1" of soil

Pruning the Plants

Know when to prune

Give most bush and tree roses their annual pruning during their dormant period before buds begin to swell on the bare canes. This can be anytime between January in warm areas and April in severe-winter climates. Prune roses that flower only once a year just after they bloom. Seasonal pruning is done whenever needed during the growing season. This includes cutting off faded blossoms before they swell into seed pods, called hips; removing diseased or broken growth; training or slowing growth; and eliminating suckers.

| January | February | March | April |

| May | June | July | August |

| September | October | November | December |

Annual Pruning
January: mild climates
February/March: cold winter climates
April: severe winter climates

Seasonal Pruning
May–December

Decide where to cut

When pruning, wear gloves and use sharp, clean, well-lubricated tools, such as hand-pruning shears, long-handled lopping shears (for thick canes), and a fine-toothed curved saw for cutting woody canes. Cut stems at a sharp, 30- to 45-degree angle, about ⅛ to ¼ inch above the bud. This angle allows water to run off instead of collecting on the wound. If you cut too high, you will leave a stub above the bud where the wood will die, providing an entrance for pests and diseases.

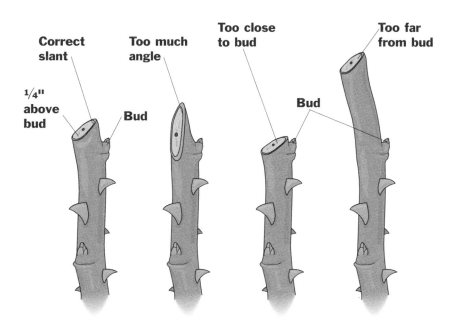

Correct slant

Too much angle

Too close to bud

Too far from bud

¼" above bud

Bud

Bud

Bud

T I P : If hips remain on the canes, flowering stops.

You should usually cut to a bud that points up and away from the crown or center of the bush. Pruning directs growth, and roses should be encouraged to form an open-centered, vase-shaped plant. If they tend to sprawl too widely, prune to an inward-facing bud, which will cause the plant to be fuller and more bushy. When using pruning shears, ensure a clean cut by positioning the thin blade of the shears just above the bud.

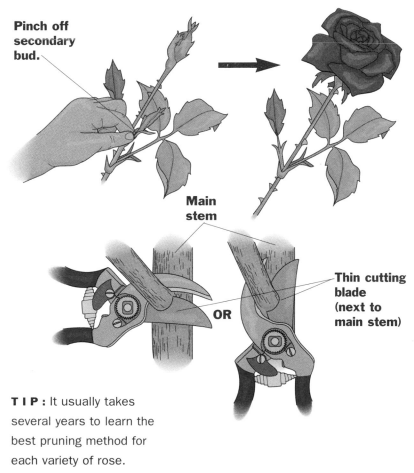

Pinch off secondary bud.

Main stem

Thin cutting blade (next to main stem)

OR

TIP: It usually takes several years to learn the best pruning method for each variety of rose.

Prune bush roses

3

Completely remove any dead, diseased, thin, or twiggy shoots. Remove frost-damaged portions of canes by cutting back far enough to find a white or creamy color in the center. Use a saw to remove large canes. Thin out any weak or crossing shoots from the center of the bush, removing them all the way to their source, leaving no stubs. Remove any suckers by digging soil away until you can see where they are connected to the trunk; pull downward to break them off.

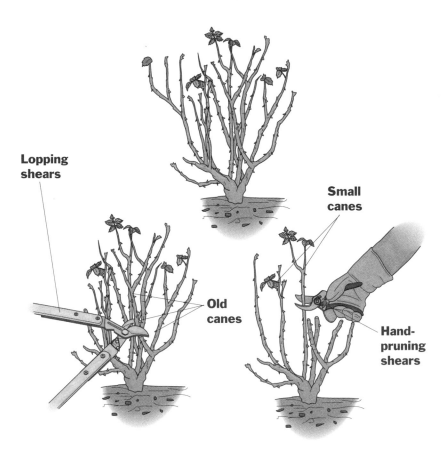

Lopping shears

Small canes

Old canes

Hand-pruning shears

The amount of growth you remove depends on how much wood was damaged by winter cold, how large you want the plant to grow, and what size and quantity of flowers you want. Pruning a plant back heavily, leaving three or four canes 8 to 10 inches high, produces fewer but showier blooms and stimulates weak plants. Moderate pruning leaves five to eight canes 18 to 24 inches high that develop into a larger bush with smaller but numerous flowers. Light pruning—cutting back less than one third of the plant—produces more but smaller flowers and larger-growing plants.

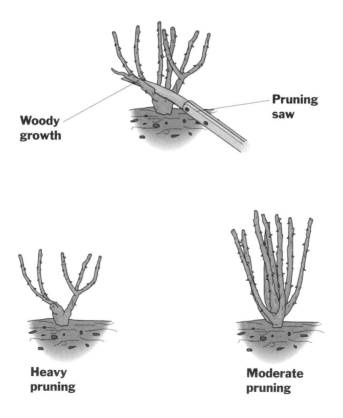

Woody growth

Pruning saw

Heavy pruning

Moderate pruning

Cut back climbers

Do not prune climbers for the first two years, except to cut out any dead, diseased, or weak, twiggy growth. After that, climbers that bloom only once a year should be pruned in the fall after they have flowered. Cut out diseased canes and remove older, gray canes as well as weak new ones. To shape the plant, save the green, healthy canes and cut back the laterals, on which the flowers appear, to four or five sets of leaves. Remove any suckers from the base of the plant (see page 44).

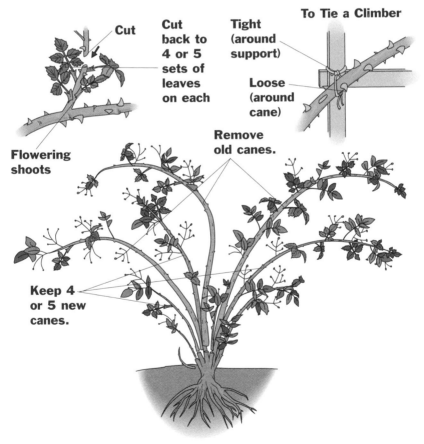

Cut

Cut back to 4 or 5 sets of leaves on each

Tight (around support)

To Tie a Climber

Loose (around cane)

Flowering shoots

Remove old canes.

Keep 4 or 5 new canes.

Once-blooming climbers
(supports left out to show pruning)

Prune climbing hybrid tea roses and everblooming large-flowered climbers when dormant in late winter or early spring. Remove dead and diseased canes, suckers, and old or weak growth. Keep three or four vigorous young canes, and cut back the lateral shoots to two leaf buds. Pick off faded blossoms from everblooming climbers but do not take any foliage; the next blooms grow from the leaves right under the old flowers. When removing blooms from climbing hybrid teas, leave two sets of leaves on each flowering shoot.

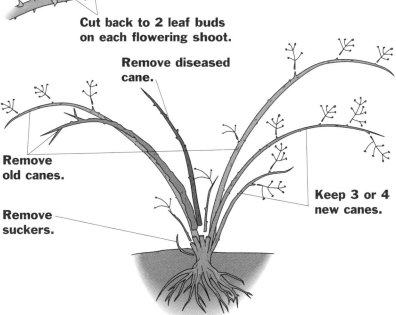

Cut back to 2 leaf buds
on each flowering shoot.

Remove diseased
cane.

Remove
old canes.

Remove
suckers.

Keep 3 or 4
new canes.

Climbing hybrid teas, everbloomers
(supports left out to show pruning)

Shape tree varieties

Prune tree roses as you would bush roses. Thin out the top of the plant, removing dead, diseased, or twiggy canes. Prune back healthy canes by approximately one half to two thirds, so they are all roughly equal in length. Keep the shape as symmetrical as possible so the foliage will fill out full and round. Remove any suckers from the rootstock or trunk, pulling them off as close to the base as possible. Check that the support stake is in good condition and is not rubbing the plant.

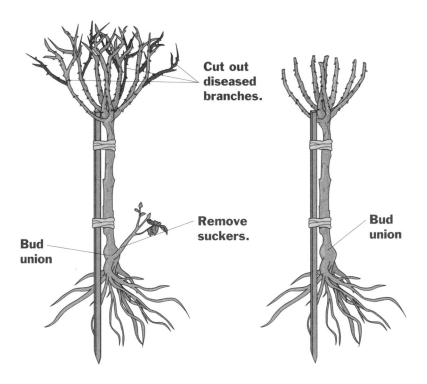

Cut out diseased branches.

Remove suckers.

Bud union

Bud union

6 Prune container plants

Prune bush roses growing in containers the same way you would those growing in a bed. Because the buds on these roses are so small, it is difficult to prune to a side bud, so reduce the plant by about one half and concentrate on cleaning it up. Leave several healthy canes growing in a symmetrical shape, and cut out accumulated twiggy growth, crossing branches, and any dead or diseased wood. Cut the canes to outside buds to encourage a well-shaped plant with an uncrowded center.

Using Roses as Cut Flowers

Pick flowers in the early morning or late afternoon. Select ones that are just opening or that have opened halfway. Use sharp shears and cut at a 45-degree angle just above a five-leaflet leaf. Put the stems into water right away and keep the flowers in a cool place. Before arranging, remove all foliage and thorns that will be below water level in the vase, and recut each stem at a sharp angle.

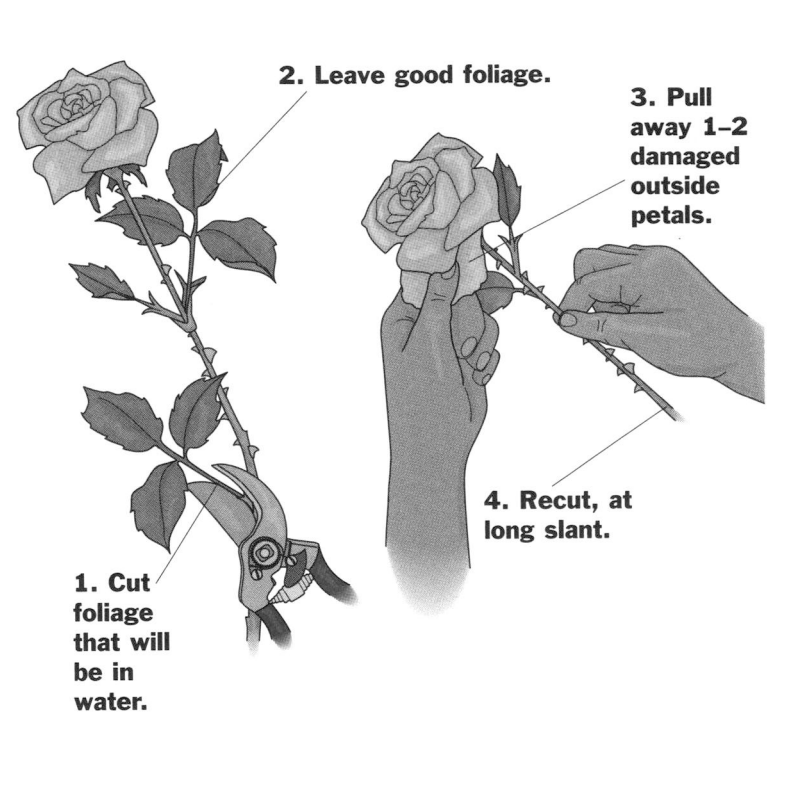

2. Leave good foliage.

3. Pull away 1–2 damaged outside petals.

4. Recut, at long slant.

1. Cut foliage that will be in water.

Fill a vase with fresh water. Use a commercial floral preserv-
ative or one teaspoon of household bleach for every quart
of water to keep the flowers fresh longer. Keep the roses in
as cool a place as possible, out of drafts and direct sunlight.
Add enough fresh water daily to keep the stems immersed
up to two thirds of their length. Recut the bottom of the
stems every day or so.

A Glossary of Rose Terms

Anchor roots Heavy roots that serve primarily to stabilize the plant.

Bare root A dormant plant without soil around its roots. Roses are most often sold this way.

Bicolor A rose of two colors, usually one on the front or inside and one on the petal back.

Bud A developing flower or the point on a stem from which new stem growth will begin. See *eye*.

Bud union The swollen stem section at or near soil level where the bud of the top variety was grafted to the rootstock.

Cane One of the main stems of a rosebush. They originate at or very near the bud union.

Crown The bud union where roots join with the canes at and just above the soil level. Also, the top portion of a tree rose.

Dead heading Removal of spent blooms during the growing season to encourage more flowers.

Dieback When a cane or stem dies back to a bud or another stem because of a pruning wound.

Disbudding Removing secondary buds on a main flowering stem to divert energy they would absorb back to the main flower. Must be done while the secondary buds are quite small.

Eye A bud on a stem from which new stem growth will emerge.

Feeder roots Tiny roots that absorb water and nutrients.

Foliar feeding Applying soluble, nonburning fertilizers directly to the leaves.

Fungicide A chemical used to prevent or combat fungus diseases.

Heel in To temporarily cover the roots of a bare-root rose with damp soil or sawdust until it can be planted.

Hip The fruit of roses. It ripens to orange or red in the fall and is known for its vitamin C content.

Insecticide A chemical used to control insect pests.

Lateral A stem originating from a main cane.

Leaf A rose leaf is composed of smaller units called leaflets, and is attached to the stem just below an eye.

Leaflet One part of a leaf. Most roses have five or seven per leaf; some have as few as three. Leaflets are always arranged in opposite pairs with one at the tip.

Rootstock The species or variety rose used as the root system for the flowering top variety.

Standard A bush rose grafted to an upright stock. (Another name for a tree rose.)

Stub The end of a cane that remains after pruning. Occurs when the pruning cut was not close enough to a bud or eye, or to a cane or lateral.

Sublateral A stem that originates from a lateral.

Sucker A shoot arising from below the bud union. Its leaves, thorns, and perhaps stem color will be different. Remove as close to its point of origin as possible.

Rosa foetida persiana

Blanc Double de Coubert

ROSES FOR SPECIAL PURPOSES

On the following pages are lists of roses that are particularly recommended for fragrance, cut flowers, and other special purposes.

Key to Abbreviations

Cl   Climber

F   Floribunda

Gr   Grandiflora

HT   Hybrid Tea

M   Miniature

MS   Modern Shrub

OGR   Old Garden Rose

Sp   Species

ROSES FOR SCREENS

Altissimo (Cl)

America (Cl)

Blaze (Cl)

City of York (Cl)

Clair Matin (Cl)

Communis (OGR)

Constance Spry (MS)

Crested Moss (OGR)

Don Juan (Cl)

Dortmund (MS)

Félicité et Perpétué (OGR)

Folklore (HT)

Fred Loads (Cl)

Frühlingsgold (OGR)

Galway Bay (Cl)

Golden Showers (Cl)

Harison's Yellow (OGR)

Kathleen (MS)

Mermaid (OGR)

New Dawn (Cl)

Paul's Scarlet Climber (Cl)

Rosa banksiae (Sp)

Rosa eglanteria (Sp)

Rosa foetida persiana (Sp)

Rosa hugonis (Sp)

Rosa laevigata (Sp)

Rosa moyesii (Sp)

Sombreuil (OGR)

Sparrieshoop (MS)

Stanwell Perpetual (OGR)

Sunny June (MS)

ROSES FOR HEDGES

All That Jazz (MS)

Blanc Double de Coubert (MS)

Carefree Wonder (MS)

Altissimo

Dicky (F)

Duet (HT)

Europeana (F)

Eyepaint (F)

Frau Dagmar Hartopp (MS)

H. C. Andersen (F)

Iceberg (F)

Madame Hardy (OGR)

Meidomonac (Bonica '82) (MS)

Old Blush (OGR)

Pink Grootendorst (MS)

Queen Elizabeth (Gr)

Rosa rugosa (Sp)

Sexy Rexy (F)

Showbiz (F)

Simplicity (F)

**ROSES FOR
GROUND COVERS**

Dortmund (MS)

Félicité et Perpétué (OGR)

Ferdinand Pichard (OGR)

New Dawn (Cl)

Red Cascade (M)

Rosa laevigata (Sp)

Rosa spinosissima (Sp)

Rosa wichuraiana (Sp)

Dublin

ROSES BY COLOR

Red Roses

Altissimo (CL)

Beauty Secret (M)

Black Jade (M)

Blaze (Cl)

Chrysler Imperial (HT)

Crimson Glory (HT)

Don Juan (Cl)

Dortmund (MS)

Dublin (HT)

Esperanza (F)

Europeana (F)

Eyepaint (F)

Ferdinand Pichard (OGR)

Général Jacqueminot (OGR)

H. C. Andersen (F)

Korlingo (F)

Loving Memory (HT)

Mister Lincoln (HT)

Olympiad (HT)

Papa Meilland (HT)

Paul's Scarlet Climber (Cl)

Precious Platinum (HT)

Red Cascade (M)

Rosa moyesii (Sp)

Carefree Wonder

Scarlet Knight (Gr)
Showbiz (F)
Swarthmore (HT)
Trojan Victory (HT)
Uncle Joe (HT)

Pink Roses

America (Cl)
Apothecary's Rose (OGR)
Aquarius (Gr)
Autumn Damask (OGR)
Baronne Prévost (OGR)
Betty Prior (F)
Bewitched (HT)
Brigadoon (HT)
Carefree Wonder (MS)
Celestial (OGR)
Charlotte Armstrong (HT)
Cherish (F)
Clair Matin (Cl)
Climbing Cécile Brünner (Cl)
Communis (OGR)
Complicata (OGR)
Confidence (HT)
Constance Spry (MS)
Crested Moss (OGR)

Delicate

Cupcake (M)
Delicate (MS)
Duchesse de Brabant (OGR)
Electron (HT)
Fantin-Latour (OGR)
First Prize (HT)
Frau Dagmar Hartopp (MS)
Gene Boerner (F)
Great Scott (HT)
Hermosa (OGR)
Honorine de Brabant (OGR)
Jennifer (M)
Kathleen (MS)
Keepsake (HT)
Königin von Dänemark (OGR)
La Reine Victoria (OGR)
Maman Cochet (OGR)
Marchesa Boccella (OGR)
Meidomonac (Bonica '82) (MS)
Minnie Pearl (M)
Miss All-American Beauty (HT)
New Dawn (Cl)
Old Blush (OGR)
Perfume Delight (HT)
Pink Grootendorst (MS)
Pink Parfait (Gr)

Luis Desamero

Prima Donna (Gr)
Queen Elizabeth (Gr)
Rosa eglanteria (Sp)
Rosa virginiana (Sp)
Rose de Meaux (OGR)
Royal Highness (HT)
Secret (HT)
Sexy Rexy (F)
Sheer Elegance (HT)
Simplicity (F)
Sparrieshoop (MS)
Sweet Inspiration (F)
Tiffany (HT)
Touch of Class (HT)
Tournament of Roses (Gr)
York and Lancaster (OGR)

Lavender to Purple Roses

Angel Face (F)
Intrigue (F)
Lady X (HT)
Madame Violebrut (HT)
Paradise (HT)
Reine des Violettes (OGR)
Rosa rugosa (Sp)
Silverado (HT)

Sun Flare

Superb Tuscan (OGR)
Winsome (M)
Wise Portia (MS)

Yellow Roses

Baby Eclipse (M)
Elegance (Cl)
Elina (HT)
Frühlingsgold (OGR)
Golden Showers (Cl)
Harison's Yellow (OGR)
Helmut Schmidt (HT)
Little Darling (F)
Luis Desamero (M)
Maid of Honour (HT)
Midas Touch (HT)
My Sunshine (M)
Oregold (HT)
Party Girl (M)
Rosa banksiae (Sp)
Rosa foetida persiana (Sp)
Rosa hugonis (Sp)
Sun Flare (F)
Sunny June (MS)
Sunsprite (F)
Sutter's Gold (HT)

Caribbean

First Edition

Apricot Roses

Apricot Nectar (F)

Baby Darling (M)

Brandy (HT)

Buff Beauty (MS)

Jean Kenneally (M)

Loving Touch (M)

Royal Sunset (Cl)

Orange-Red and Orange to Gold Roses

All That Jazz (MS)

Anabell (F)

Caribbean (Gr)

Cary Grant (HT)

Dicky (F)

Dolly Parton (HT)

First Edition (F)

Folklore (HT)

Fragrant Cloud (HT)

Impatient (F)

Little Jackie (M)

Marina (F)

Mary Marshall (M)

New Beginning (M)

Olé (Gr)

Pride 'n Joy (M)

Prominent (Gr)

Solitude (Gr)

Starina (M)

Tropicana (HT)

White to Cream Roses

Blanc Double de Coubert (MS)

Child's Play (M)

Cinderella (M)

City of York (Cl)

Class Act (F)

Fair Bianca (MS)

Félicité et Perpétué (OGR)

Frau Karl Druschki (OGR)

French Lace (F)

Garden Party (HT)

Gourmet Popcorn (M)

Great Maiden's Blush (OGR)

Honor (HT)

Iceberg (F)

Ivory Fashion (F)

Koricole (F)

Kristin (M)

Lamarque (OGR)

Madame Hardy (OGR)

Miyabi (HT)

Granada

Nana Mouskouri (F)
Nevada (MS)
Pacesetter (M)
Pascali (HT)
Pelé (Cl)
Pristine (HT)
Rosa banksiae (Sp)
Rosa laevigata (Sp)
Rosa spinosissima (Sp)
Rosa wichuraiana (Sp)
Sheer Bliss (HT)
Snow Bride (M)
Sombreuil (OGR)
Souvenir de la Malmaison (OGR)
Stanwell Perpetual (OGR)
Summer Fashion (F)
White Dawn (Cl)
White Masterpiece (HT)
White Success (HT)

Bicolor and Multicolor Roses

Chicago Peace (HT)
Color Magic (HT)
Double Delight (HT)
Dreamglo (M)
Granada (HT)

Rio Samba

Holy Toledo (M)
Joseph's Coat (Cl)
Love (Gr)
Mikado (HT)
Mon Cheri (HT)
Osiria (HT)
Peace (HT)
Peaches 'n Cream (M)
Perfect Moment (HT)
Rainbow's End (M)
Redgold (F)
Rio Samba (HT)
Rosa foetida bicolor (Sp)
Rosa Mundi (OGR)
Toy Clown (M)
Voodoo (HT)

ESPECIALLY FRAGRANT ROSES

Angel Face (F)
Apothecary's Rose (OGR)
Autumn Damask (OGR)
Beauty Secret (M)
Bewitched (HT)
Blanc Double de Coubert (MS)
Bride's Dream (HT)
Captain Harry Stebbings (HT)

Folklore

Child's Play (M)
Chrysler Imperial (HT)
City of York (Cl)
Communis (OGR)
Confidence (HT)
Crimson Glory (HT)
Dolly Parton (HT)
Don Juan (Cl)
Double Delight (HT)
Dublin (HT)
Duchesse de Brabant (OGR)
Folklore (HT)
Fragrant Cloud (HT)
Général Jacqueminot (OGR)
Granada (HT)
Honorine de Brabant (OGR)
Iceberg (F)
Intrigue (F)
Keepsake (HT)
Königin von Dänemark (OGR)
Little Darling (F)
Madame Hardy (OGR)
Nana Mouskouri (F)
Pacesetter (M)
Papa Meilland (HT)
Perfume Delight (HT)

Fragrant Cloud

Pierrine (M)
Pride 'n Joy (M)
Rosa laevigata (Sp)
Rosa rugosa (Sp)
Salet (OGR)
Secret (HT)
Sombreuil (OGR)
Sonia (Gr)
Sunsprite (F)
Sutter's Gold (HT)
Tiffany (HT)

LONG-LASTING CUT ROSES

Anabell (F)
Bewitched (HT)
Brigadoon (HT)
Captain Harry Stebbings (HT)
Cary Grant (HT)
Century Two (HT)
Chrysler Imperial (HT)
Cupcake (M)
Dicky (F)
Dolly Parton (HT)
Double Delight (HT)
Dublin (HT)
Elina (HT)

Maid of Honour

Elizabeth Taylor (HT)
First Edition (F)
First Prize (HT)
Folklore (HT)
Garden Party (HT)
Great Scott (HT)
Jean Kenneally (M)
Korlingo (HT)
Kristin (M)
Lady X (HT)
Little Darling (F)
Love (Gr)
Maid of Honour (HT)
Marina (F)
Mister Lincoln (HT)
Mon Cheri (HT)
Paradise (HT)
Pascali (HT)
Peace (HT)
Peaches 'n Cream (M)
Pierrine (M)
Precious Platinum (HT)
Prominent (Gr)
Royal Highness (HT)
Sheer Elegance (HT)
Silverado (HT)

Bewitched

Sonia (Gr)
Starina (M)
Suffolk (HT)
Swarthmore (HT)
Tiffany (HT)
Touch of Class (HT)
Trojan Victory (HT)
Tropicana (HT)
Uncle Joe (HT)
White Masterpiece (HT)

HARDIEST MODERN ROSES

Bewitched (HT)
Black Jade (M)
Blanc Double de Coubert (MS)
Captain Harry Stebbings (HT)
Carefree Wonder (MS)
City of York (Cl)
Crimson Glory (HT)
Dicky (F)
Dortmund (MS)
Dublin (HT)
Elina (HT)
Europeana (F)
Eyepaint (F)
Folklore (HT)

First Prize

Nevada

Frau Dagmar Hartopp (MS)
Garden Party (HT)
Gold Medal (Gr)
Golden Wings (MS)
Great Scott (HT)
H. C. Andersen (F)
Iceberg (F)
Jean Kenneally (M)
Jennifer (M)
Kathleen (MS)
Koricole (F)
Lady X (HT)
Little Darling (F)
Loving Memory (HT)
Maid of Honour (HT)
Marijke Koopman (HT)
Meidomonac (Bonica '82) (MS)
Nevada (MS)
Pacesetter (M)
Pink Grootendoorst (MS)
Precious Platinum (HT)
Suffolk (HT)
Swarthmore (HT)
Trojan Victory (HT)
Uncle Joe (HT)

MOST DISEASE-RESISTANT ROSES

Bride's Dream (HT)
Brigadoon (HT)
Carefree Wonder (MS)
City of York (Cl)
Confidence (HT)
Dicky (F)
Dortmund (MS)
Dublin (HT)
Elina (HT)
First Prize (HT)
Folklore (HT)
Gold Medal (Gr)
Great Scott (HT)
H. C. Andersen (F)
Keepsake (HT)
Koricole (F)
Korlingo (HT)
Maid of Honour (HT)
Marijke Koopman (HT)
Meidomonac (Bonica '82) (MS)
Miyabi (HT)
Olympiad (HT)
Osiria (HT)
Pink Parfait (Gr)
Precious Platinum (HT)

Pristine

Tropicana

Pristine (HT)
Sheer Elegance (HT)
Suffolk (HT)
Trojan Victory (HT)
Uncle Joe (HT)
White Success (HT)

EASIEST-TO-GROW ROSES
Beauty Secret (M)
Betty Prior (F)
Bewitched (HT)
Blaze (Cl)
Cherish (F)
City of York (Cl)
Dicky (F)
Dortmund (MS)
Dublin (HT)
Duet (HT)
Elina (HT)
Europeana (F)
First Prize (HT)
Folklore (HT)
Fragrant Cloud (HT)
Garden Party (HT)
Gold Medal (Gr)
Great Scott (HT)

H. C. Andersen (F)
Harison's Yellow (OGR)
Iceberg (F)
Koricole (F)
Korlingo (HT)
Kristin (M)
Little Darling (F)
Magic Carrousel (M)
Maid of Honour (HT)
Meidomonac (Bonica '82) (MS)
Minnie Pearl (M)
Mister Lincoln (HT)
Miyabi (HT)
Pacesetter (M)
Pristine (HT)
Queen Elizabeth (Gr)
Rainbow's End (M)
Rise 'n Shine (M)
Rosa eglanteria (Sp)
Snow Bride (M)
Suffolk (HT)
Trojan Victory (HT)
Tropicana (HT)

U.S./Metric Measure Conversions

Formulas for Exact Measures

Rounded Measures for Quick Reference

	Symbol	When you know:	Multiply by:	To find:		
Mass	oz	ounces	28.35	grams	1 oz	= 30 g
(Weight)	lb	pounds	0.45	kilograms	4 oz	= 115 g
	g	grams	0.035	ounces	8 oz	= 225 g
	kg	kilograms	2.2	pounds	16 oz	= 1 lb = 450 g
					32 oz	= 2 lb = 900 g
					36 oz	= $2^1/_4$ lb = 1000 g (1 kg)
Volume	pt	pints	0.47	liters	1 c	= 8 oz = 250 ml
	qt	quarts	0.95	liters	2 c (1pt)	= 16 oz = 500 ml
	gal	gallons	3.785	liters	4 c (1 qt)	= 32 oz = 1 liter
	ml	milliliters	0.034	fluid ounces	4 qt (1 gal)	= 128 oz = $3^3/_4$ liter
Length	in.	inches	2.54	centimeters	$^3/_8$ in.	= 1.0 cm
	ft	feet	30.48	centimeters	1 in.	= 2.5 cm
	yd	yards	0.9144	meters	2 in.	= 5.0 cm
	mi	miles	1.609	kilometers	$2^1/_2$ in.	= 6.5 cm
	km	kilometers	0.621	miles	12 in. (1 ft)	= 30.0 cm
	m	meters	1.094	yards	1 yd	= 90.0 cm
	cm	centimeters	0.39	inches	100 ft	= 30.0 m
					1 mi	= 1.6 km
Temperature	°F	Fahrenheit	$^5/_9$ (after subtracting 32)	Celsius	32° F	= 0° C
	°C	Celsius	$^9/_5$ (then add 32)	Fahrenheit	212° F	= 100° C
Area	in.²	square inches	6.452	square centimeters	1 in.²	= 6.5 cm²
	ft²	square feet	929.0	square centimeters	1 ft²	= 930 cm²
	yd²	square yards	8361.0	square centimeters	1 yd²	= 8360 cm²
	a.	acres	0.4047	hectares	1 a.	= 4050 m²